Conquering Holiday Grief
(with journaling pages)

©1999 by Patty Harris
 ISBN 978-0-9669849-3-4
Published by Grief Relief Publishing Co., Inc.
Printed in the United States of America.
All scripture references are from the King James Version of the Holy Bible.

Lovingly dedicated to each of you who
for the past 30 years
have confidentially shared and trusted me
with your tears, sorrows, joys,
heartaches, and vulnerabilities
that occur during the
healing journey of grief and mourning.
Whether I was your Pastor,
hospital chaplain, confidante,
or friend - I love each of you!
Grace and Peace,

Pastor Patty

CONTENTS

My Christmas is With Jesus

I see the countless Christmas trees
Around the world below
With tiny lights like heaven's stairs,
Reflecting on the snow!

The sight is so spectacular,
Please wipe away the tear
For I am spending Christmas...
With Jesus Christ this year!

I know the many Christmas songs
That people hold so dear
But the sounds of music can't compare...
With the Hallelujah choir up here!

I have no words to tell you
The joy their voices bring,
For it is beyond description,
To hear the angels sing.

I know how much you miss me,
There is pain inside your heart,
But I am not so far away
We really aren't apart...
So be happy for me, loved ones,
You know I hold you dear,
And rejoice that I'm spending Christmas...
With Jesus Christ this year!

I sent you each a special gift
From my heavenly home above,
I sent you each a memory...
Of my undying love.

After all...
Love is a gift more precious
More precious than pure gold,
It was always most important
In the stories Jesus told.

Please love and keep each other,
As our Heavenly Father said to do
For I can't count the blessing of love...
He has for each of you.

So have a Merry Christmas...
As you wipe away that tear
Remember....
I am spending Christmas...
With Jesus Christ this year!!!
(Author Unknown)

INTRODUCTION

The God of the Bible is the Healer of the brokenhearted!!! The brokenhearted are those who are deeply distressed and in sorrow or trouble of any kind. Jesus tells us in Luke 4:18c "... *He hath sent Me to heal the brokenhearted* ... "

The Bible does not shy away from the reality of grief and the need for healing. When we read in Matthew 27, we find that Jesus did not want to drink of the cup of suffering. In His humanity He didn't want to endure the pain and grief that awaited Him at Calvary. How like us was our Savior! Each of us will at some time in life have our Gethsemane to Golgotha experience.

We will experience a place so alone, so heavy, so dark, so tearful that we feel no one else understands. Jesus understands the anguish of the sorrow of grief. Even Jesus needed help to carry His cross! He will bear this with you as you walk through this valley of grief. The Bible does not assure us of the absence of grief in life, it does however, promise us the Presence of God.

As Christians, we know and believe that we will see our loved ones again and look forward to the celebration and reunion (I Thessalonians 4:13-18). However, between now and then we will miss our loved ones while we are still here on earth.

Yea, though I walk through the valley of the shadow of death, I will fear no evil: for Thou art with me; Thy rod and Thy staff they comfort me.
Psalms 23:4

What is Grief?

Grief is the *emotional or mental suffering or distress over affliction or loss.* It is a natural response to any significant loss. Loss is the severance or detachment from something or someone of value.

Grief is emotional not intellectual this is why it can't be reasoned away. It will be felt. We attend to physical wounds with great care yet often neglect the emotional wounds that life inflicts upon us. The emotional wound of grief and sorrow can leave us bleeding and almost lifeless if we don't care for ourselves and be cared for by others who understand.

The grieving process is a healing one. The journey through it is life changing. The emotions are raw and varied, often intense and sometimes overwhelming. Although grief is uninvited, it occupies a room in our heart and life and is never in a hurry to leave, which is why we must learn what we can to get through it, be healed, and continue in life. Otherwise, grief will consume us and rob us of the best of who we can become!

Know that you will get through this season of mourning and grieving. Your tears will once again turn to laughter and your mourning will be turned into dancing. Your joy will return. Life will still be good. It has been changed, however it will still be good. You will not always feel intense pain and anguish. You will heal!!! It takes time and lots of love - but you will heal.

There is a time to Mourn

There is ... a time to weep, and a time to laugh; a time to mourn, and a time to dance: Eccl.3:4

Mourning is both normal and scriptural. This word mourn in the Old Testament means to tear the hair and/ or beat the breast (which was customary throughout the Bible) to express grief. Throughout the Bible we are given examples of those who mourned.

Mourning is the season of adapting to loss or a change in life. It is that healing season of transition and adjustment to life without the physical presence of our loved one. (This is taught more fully in the author's book: *Blessed are they that Mourn*). Learning to understand grief can help us to ease holiday stress associated with it. It won't take away all the pain, but it will help to ease the burden.

Grief and mourning are often used interchangeably, however, there is a slight difference. While grief is the intense emotional suffering and anguish caused by loss, death, or misfortune, to mourn is the expression of that grief as well as the time of transition and adjustment.

This process of mourning begins as we start to emerge from the painful experience of shock and denial of the death. This is when we begin the task of rebuilding our life without the physical presence of a loved one. We begin to feel the loss at every aspect of our life. However, the pain is not hidden inwardly, it is acknowledged, it is felt, and it is expressed.

This does not mean that the tears will not flow or that the pain and sorrow has ended. It means we have reached a mindset that we know we must rebuild our life in the midst of tears and heartache! This is what makes mourning a time of healing. It is in this painful time of transition and adjustment that healing begins to take place.

Conquering Holiday Grief

It's that joyful time of year again!

The Thanksgiving/Christmas holiday season. The word *'holiday'* itself means *a celebration!* Webster's dictionary defines *'holiday'* as *a day fixed by law or custom on which ordinary business is suspended in commemoration of some event or in honor of some person; a joyous and festive occasion.*

During this holiday season there are pretty bows, bright lights, silver bells, cornucopias, garland, and mistletoe to name a few things that make this season more festive. There is much laughter and a lot of hustle and bustle.

Even nature call for the leaves on the trees to add beauty all around us. The leaves on the trees change from green to pretty vibrant and various shades of orange, yellow, red, gold, and brown. Thanksgiving decorations are on one side of the mall and Christmas decorations are on the other. It is impossible to avoid the festive impact of this holiday season.

It's beginning to look a lot like Christmas!

The sights! The sounds! Good will to everyone. Joy abounds! Everything looks, sounds, and smells so good! However, even in the midst of the glorious season of Thanksgiving sentiment, Christmas cheer, and the bright lights, there will still be some people who inwardly find it difficult to enjoy the holiday as they once did because they are grappling with grief, particularly over the death of a loved one.

For some, the holidays are now a painful reminder that the gift giving which has been so much fun, is now so full of sadness. Many people would prefer to skip the last three months of the calendar year altogether.

Everyone experiences some type of grief in life. Whether it is the death of a loved one, an unwanted divorce which means the death of a marriage and the disintegration of a family, the loss of a job, the loss of a pet ... the list goes on. Grief is not abnormal and it is certainly nothing to be ashamed of. Being a Christian does not exempt us from the sorrow of grief, however, it does give us a Savior, a Comforter to help us walk through this valley.

Sorrow, pain, and tragedy were not a part of God's plan for us. These came after the Fall of man. They came from the enemy as a result of sin and disobedience. However, on the Cross of Calvary, Jesus Christ provided a way for addressing as well as conquering these issues in life.

There is a great exchange that will take place as we experience the healing process of grief. Comfort is what God has provided for our season of grief and mourning. God has promised to give us beauty for ashes, the oil of joy for our mourning. He will replace our spirit of heaviness with a garment of praise.

Comfort is what God gives in the midst of our mourning. It is God's divine will that each of us be comforted, that we comfort one another, and that we be healed.

Blessed be God, even the Father of our Lord Jesus Christ, the Father of mercies, and the God of all comfort; 4 Who comforteth us in all our tribulation, that we may be able to comfort them which are in any trouble, by the comfort wherewith we ourselves are comforted of God.
II Corinthians 1:3-4

He sent his word, and healed them, and delivered them from their destructions. Psalms 107:20

It is frustrating and awkward coping with bittersweet emotions during this time of the year. The bright lights seem a little dim at times; happiness is mixed with sorrow of heart; and quite often tears of joy that the season brings are intermingled with tears of sorrow from the heart. This is normal. In the midst of pain and grief it is sometimes difficult to enjoy the beautiful sights and sounds as you once did. Even if surrounded by family and friends you might still feel as if no one understands your inner turmoil.

For people experiencing this type of bereavement, the holiday season takes on a different meaning. The holiday season can be a painful reminder of the loss you are feeling. Quite often, the first few years are the most difficult. You do not have to pretend that everything is okay and perfectly normal. It is not! Your life has been forever changed. The death of a loved one creates a void.

Adapting to the death of a loved one is quite difficult, especially during the holidays. This time of year has a tendency to intensify feelings of loneliness and yearnings for the loved one. The pain you feel is an indication that you love! Your life has been touched by another.

The leaves on the trees seem to coincide with our emotions - varied. Our feelings go from being bright and joyful to dull and listless. But just as the seasons change in time, so will the hurting places in your heart. The deep intense pain will diminish. This does not mean that the love you have for your loved one is gone, it only means that you are healing!

You will get through the holiday season - all of them. Not just the Thanksgiving/Christmas season, but the birthdays, anniversaries, and other memorable days. It will take time, love, and care but you will get through it. You will outlive the pain of your grief.

Holiday grief often serves as a milestone in our emotional survival. We are reminded *of "How long it has been since ... "* or *"This is the first, second, or even the tenth holiday without my loved one."* So many experiences will trigger memories of past holidays with your loved one.

Confronting the holiday season seems to be just that - a confrontation. But if there is no confrontation there can be no conquering and if there is no conquering there will be no resolution and without resolution, there will be no growth. Every confrontation brings along with it a challenge to grow and be strengthened. This happens as we put our trust in the God of all strength who has promised to never leave us nor forsake us - especially in the most difficult circumstances.

The anguish and pain of grief runs deep and affects us in every aspect of our life. If you are grieving the loss of a loved one, unfortunately the pain doesn't stop when you return to work. The pain is still in your heart. This is why it is a process to get through grief. Grief is with you everywhere you go because it is within you.

Whether you go to the store, Church, or work, grief is there. If you suppress the feelings and emotions that are associated with grief, the pain is still there lying underneath the activities that are chosen to suppress the pain. The pain will still be within the deep places of your heart until you deal with it.

At a time when there is usually much love shared, many thanks are given, this is also a time that reminds us that the circle has been broken. During the holidays especially we grieve the person who has died as well as the loss of the time we will no longer be able to share with the loved one.

Our physical relationship and closeness has now turned to cherished memories. We reminisce about the past and quite often desire for things to be the way they were before. We find ourselves mentally and emotionally reviewing conversations and happy times that have been shared. These moments can help us to smile through the difficult emotional times or some days they can bring on more tears. Either way it is still a milestone in the process of healing.

This type of suffering and grief is a part of life that no one is exempt from and being a Christian does not erase the pain that is felt. Even as Christians we must realize that grief is not something we have to hide or be ashamed of for experiencing.

Our faith is at its highest when we seem at our lowest and are simply trusting God to carry us through a difficult season of bereavement. Jesus told His disciples He was going away but that He would send them another Comforter. We have this same Comforter, the Holy Spirit who dwells within us to guide us through the storms of life called grief. The Holy Spirit will bring peace into our minds and heart.

It may seem difficult to understand at first but there will be a time when you will be able to look back over this season and see that one set of *"Footprints"* and know that it was Jesus who carried you through.

Grief was something that Jesus knew was an important issue so He took the time to prepare His disciples (and us) for the pain and suffering that would be faced in the world. He did promise that because He overcame we too would have power to overcome.

The pain and anguish of grief is something that we can and will conquer as we put our trust in God. During holiday grief there is often an inclination to avoid the festivities of the holidays by becoming detached and socially isolated from others. Emotions may range from feeling angry to feeling happy; from joy to sorrow; hope to hopelessness; feeling angry at God to feeling angry at the one who has died; to feeling angry at self; to feeling angry at others for enjoying the holiday season.

These feelings are not irrational. In fact, they represent a normal range of emotions associated with the sorrow and pain of loss. Your emotions might waver between wanting to retreat and be alone to desperately wanting to participate in joyful holiday activities. All these varied emotional and mental reactions can be quite overwhelming!

In 1904, after struggling in her personal life and marriage, Mrs. Civilla D. Martin penned the words of a well beloved hymn which is still encouraging to us today. In times of personal sorrow and difficulty always remember:

Be not dismayed. what e' ere betide,
God will take care of you.
Beneath His wings of love abide,
God will take care of you.
God will take care of you.
Through every day,
All of the way.
He will take care of you.
God will take of you.

There is a healing process that occurs in grief. As with any process you must be actively involved to receive the best benefit of growth, change, and development. People often say "time heals all wounds". However, it is not time that heals but what you do in time that will bring healing. Time is neutral and only passes. If we are not careful or active in our healing process, we will simply sit and wait and wait for time to heal all the while possibly sinking into further despair and depression. Time itself does not heal the emotional wound of grief. It is available for us to use for healing.

We must take advantage of time in order to heal. We must be active. Healing from loss is achieved by taking a series of small steps! Yes, life has been forever changed, but it can still be meaningful and full of activity. You must choose to go forward in life - one moment at a time if this is all you can handle right now. Take that step toward activity - no matter how small it may seem.

You will realize that the smallest step isn't that small at all. It is vitally important to your emotional well-being, spiritual health, and physical vitality.

This section titled Family Matters and Grief Relief Points to Ponder are taken from the author's book *Surviving the Death of a Loved One* where they are taught in more detail.

Here are some practical things that can be done to help you understand and conquer holiday grief or grief at any time.

Family Matters:

Children are often the forgotten grievers. In trying to shield them, they are often left alone to figure things out on their own. Children should be included. Be honest and age appropriate with children. They are quite resilient.

Although they grieve differently than adults, the reactions are very similar. Children can quickly become absorbed in other activities and become distracted. However, in the next few minutes be aware of the death again. Their attention span is short and so is their emotional span. Allow them to grieve in their way. Use natural times together as opportunities to start a conversation about the death of the loved one.

Especially during the holidays, it is a good idea for families to openly express to each other how they feel. Quite often, a death will lead to internal changes within the family. These changes will often influence as well as challenge the structure of the family. Family adaptation to a loved one's death is difficult and can be even more distressing during the holiday season.

Make family decisions about how to approach the holidays. Focus on the good times previously shared with your loved one.

Talking about and remembering the death will happen from time to time. Remembering the life is also vital in the healing process. It must also be remembered that not all family members will be able to talk and/or share their memories.

Family members may be at different stages of the healing process. Because of this, each person may have his/her own expectation of how they think others should behave.

Everyone grieves a death differently. To diminish problems and conflicts, families must be careful to respect each others' grieving and healing process.

Don't be afraid to have photo albums out of past holidays with your loved one. Talking about the past and how you feel now helps bring healing (often with tears), and helps you to move into your future.

It seems difficult to face the future when the present is so painful but these small steps help make it possible.

Healing Points to Ponder:

1. Remember God is with you! Quite often when experiencing grief, it is hard to formulate words for prayer. That's okay!! [God truly understands the language within the sighing of your soul and the conversation that resides in each tear that falls! So if the best way for you to pray is to sit and cry - then pray on!!! God hears you!

2. Give yourself permission to cry. There is healing in tears for men and for women!

3. Be patient with yourself - God is! The healing journey through grief is a difficult one. Even if you have experienced loss before, you have never been on this particular road before. Go gently.

4. Read through comforting Bible Scriptures.

5. Give yourself permission to laugh and enjoy life. Don't allow bitterness or guilt because you are alive to consume you and rob you of the ability to laugh and still enjoy life.

6. Try not to compare yourself to other people who have experienced grief. Grief is different for everyone. No two people grieve the same. Although there are similarities and things that are common in the grieving process, the healing process of grief is unique and unlike any other life experience.

Someone may look fine on the outside and we think he/she is handling the pain of grief quite well, however, no one knows the inner turmoil that a person is grappling with in the midst of sorrow. Don't look on the outward appearance of another to gauge yourself.

7. Ask for and receive help as well as comfort. It is not a sign of weakness, but a sign of strength to ask for help. Ask God to bring someone to you who is willing to walk with you through this valley. God is always with you and God understands that at times we need God clothed in humanity with us!

8. Pray! Never underestimate the power of prayer of God's willingness and ability to answer you. If it is still too difficult to pray this is okay. God understands the language of the sighing of a broken heart, and the language of tears speaks volumes to a caring and loving Heavenly Father. Your tears will be your prayers!

9. Be good to yourself. Get adequate rest.

10. Be aware of physical reactions to your loss. It may be good to visit your physician for a check-up after the death of a loved one. Your entire being: Spirit, soul, and body is sorting through the emotional wreckage that the death of a loved one causes. So you are in a season of regaining emotional, spiritual, and physical equilibrium. This can take a toll on one's health.

Here are some things that are common in the grieving process:

Physical Sensations:
Hollowness in stomach
Breathlessness
Tightness in chest and/or throat
Weakness in muscles
Lack of energy
Dry mouth
Physical pain
Headache
Nausea

Behaviors:

Lack of appetite
Overeating
Social withdrawal
Sighing
Crying
Unable to sleep
Sleeping too much
Forgetfulness
Trembling

Feelings:

Fear
Abandonment
Despair
Anxiety
Loneliness
Fatigue
Numbness
Depression
Shock
Helplessness
Hopelessness

<u>Cognitions:</u>

Disbelief
Confusion
Hallucinations

Although some of these symptoms of grief are common, you may or may not experience some of them. It is always good to let your physician know when you have suffered the death of a loved one.

11. Try not to completely detach or isolate yourself from family and friends. Although there will be times when you need to be alone with God and meditate or simply 'be' in His presence, it can become easy to just avoid people. Find comfort in the people who love and care for you.

12. If you are angry, even angry at God - tell God. God can handle it!! The love God has for you far outweighs any anger you could feel toward God. God will still love and care for you and be with you in the midst of this painful situation. Trust God.

13. Know that the way out of grief is through it! One's healing process through grief should not be denied. Grief will not go away simply because we refuse to acknowledge the pain. If you continually keep too busy to face your feelings and try to avoid the pain, you may be subjecting yourself to a higher risk of illness.

14. Understand that grief isn't entirely negative. It does give us the opportunity to grow and puts within us a spiritual and emotional understanding and compassion that can't be learned from a textbook. There are some things in life that only grief and heartache can teach us. There is a healing that takes place within us as we mourn. We learn about life, ourselves, others, and a loving God.

15. Begin a Journal. Begin to keep a daily journal of your journey through grief. Allow your thoughts and feelings to flow through you to the pen and onto the paper. Don't concern yourself with making sense or even sentence structure. Just write it and date it - if this is easiest for you. It is your journal. Journal provides a way for you to express and release your thoughts and feelings.

   Write the date and time before each entry. Some suggestions to include are: what you thought about, cried over, laughed about, an event that happened that reminded you of your loved one; feelings and emotions you experienced; changes that you've noticed; personal notes to yourself. The value in journaling becomes evident to you after a month or more. In time, as you reread through your journal, you will see the progress you've made on your journey and those who have touched your life.

   To help you get started we have included a few journal pages in the back of this book. Grief Relief Ministries, Inc. will also has a Grief Relief Healing Journaling Book. Please check our website for details.

16. After you have experienced going through the healing process of grief, lovingly and with much care reach out and help someone else.

"God does not comfort us to make us comfortable, but to make us comforters." Abraham Lincoln

Practical Suggestions for the Holidays:

Although there is nothing anyone can do that can take away the sorrow that you feel, there are some options that can help ease the pain of holiday grief.

- Accept that things will be different this year. Particularly if this is the first holiday season without your loved one.

- Give yourself permission to celebrate the holidays differently. Some holiday traditions may have to be slightly altered because of your loss. Decide which ones you want to keep and which ones you will let go (whether temporarily or permanently).

- It is okay to design new traditions that will include opportunities to remember your loved one while acknowledging that your present has changed. Do what feels right and comfortable for you.

- Create and put up a holiday 'GriefWreath' to honor your loved one. You can purchase a wreath at most craft stores along with items to decorate it. Decorate the wreath with things your loved one would have liked and in his/her favorite colors. Be creative!

- Volunteer at a Soup Kitchen sometime during the holiday. Helping others is a good way to heal.

- Volunteer at a homeless shelter sometime during this holiday season.

***If you have other ideas that you have done for the holidays, please share them with us at Grief Relief Ministries, Inc. We would love to share your ideas on our website and our next 'Holiday Book.'

Email us at: Griefrelief@hotmail.com
Website: www.GriefReliefToday.net

Other Books by Patty Harris

Blessed are They that Mourn
Bible- Find - A - Word Puzzles (Vols. I-VII)
Comforting Those who Grieve
Conquering Holiday Grief
Fear Nots for Everyday
Fear Nots for Those who Grieve
God Has An APP for That!
Pray-er Points to Ponder
PrayerWalking!
Praying in the Key of "C"
Restoring the Gates of Prayer
Surviving the Death of a Loved One
The T.A.S.K.S. of the Pray-er
The Truth about Strongholds
What You Can't Lose in the Midst of Loss

Grief Relief Ministries, Inc. is a ministry that offers spiritual and emotional support and education to caregivers and those experiencing various types of grief and stress.

A monthly newsletter *Grief Relief Today* is available along with teaching CD's and DVD's, books and brochures. Grief Relief Ministries, Inc. will also assist churches in starting and maintaining a grief and bereavement outreach ministry.

Grief Relief Ministries, Inc. also facilitates healing retreats, workshops, seminars on Grief Management, Prayer, Leadership, and Spiritual Growth and Maturity.

Journaling Pages

Journaling Pages

Journaling Pages

Journaling Pages

Journaling Pages

Journaling Pages

Journaling Pages

Journaling Pages

www.ingramcontent.com/pod-product-compliance
Lightning Source LLC
Chambersburg PA
CBHW030010040426
42337CB00012BA/719